DATE DUE

AROUND THE WORLD IN...

1200

AROUND THE WORLD IN...

1200

by Alexandra F. Service and Pamela F. Service

BENCHMARK BOOKS

MARSHALL CAVENDISH
NEW YORK

*With thanks to J. Brett McClain of the Oriental Institute,
the University of Chicago, for his careful reading of the manuscript*

Benchmark Books
Marshall Cavendish Corporation
99 White Plains Road
Tarrytown, New York 10591-9001
www.marshallcavendish.com

• • •

Library of Congress Cataloging-in-Publication Data
Service, Alexandra.
1200/Alexandra F. Service and Pamela F. Service.
p. cm—(Around the world in—)
Includes bibliographical references and index.
ISBN 0-7614-1081-3 (lib. bdg.)
Summary: Surveys important occurrences in Europe, Africa,
Asia, and the Americas around the year 1200.
1. Thirteenth century—Juvenile literature. 2. Civilization, Medieval—Juvenile literature.
3. Europe—Social conditions—To1492—Juvenile literature. 4. Africa—History—Juvenile literature.
5. Indians—History—Juvenile literature. 6. Asia—History—Juvenile literature.
[1. Thirteenth century. 2. Civilization, Medieval.] I. Service, Pamela F. II. Title. III. Series.
CB355 .S47 2001   909'.2—dc21   00-046848

• • •

Printed in Italy
1 3 5 6 4 2

• • •

Book Designer: Judith Turziano
Photo Research: Rose Corbett Gordon, Mystic CT

• • •

half title: An Ethiopian miniature painting showing the retinue, or followers, of the Queen of Sheba.
title page: *Left*: Genghis Khan and his Mongol warriors in furious battle. This 16th-century painting hangs
in a palace in Teheran, Iran, today. *Right*: England's King Richard the Lion-Hearted.

• • •

CONTENTS

King John, the son of Henry II and Eleanor of Aquitaine, signs the Magna Carta in 1215. The famous document, in which the king gave up some of his power to the barons, laid the foundation for English democracy.

INTRODUCTION

The time is A.D. 1200. In Europe a royal family has founded a dynasty that will shape the future of England and France for years to come. On the plains of central Asia, a small, obscure tribe of nomads is about to explode in a burst of energy; eventually the tribe will dominate the continent as the Mongol Empire. In southern Africa great cities built of stone are thriving; they will amaze the people of later centuries. And in South America a vast system of roads and canals shapes an empire of merchants, farmers, craftspeople, and warriors.

If you could board a time machine and go back to the year 1200, these are some of the things you might witness. Most people learn about history by focusing on just one country or place. Most of the time they learn about events only from their own perspective, that is, from the point of view of their nation or heritage. This is certainly a valid way to try to understand the world, but it can also be narrow and one-sided. In this book we thought it would be interesting to take a different approach to history, by looking at events that were occurring all across the world at one period of time. Perhaps if we take this broader, "bird's-eye" view of history, all of us may be able to understand one another a little better.

So step aboard our "time machine," and get ready for a trip around the world.

EUROPE AROUND 1200

N
W   E
S

ICELAND

SCANDINAVIA

NORWAY

North Sea

Atlantic Ocean

ENGLAND
London ●

● Paris
FRANCE

☐ HENRY II'S DOMINION
☐ CHRISTIAN SPAIN
☐ MUSLIM SPAIN

AQUITAINE

Pyrenees Mountains

LEÓN
● León
CASTILE

PORTUGAL

● Toledo

MAJORCA

AL-ANDALUS
Córdoba ●   ● Granada

Mediterranean Sea

Miles
0   200   400
Kilometers
0   200   400   600

PART I

EUROPE

A traveler from modern Europe, transported back in time to the year 1200, would find many differences. But he or she would also recognize a lot.

Today only a few European nations are still ruled by kings and queens, but in 1200 that was the norm. Fewer people lived in cities than do today, but some of the great cities of modern Europe, like Paris and London, were already important in 1200. Just like today, many European countries worked together peacefully, trading goods and influencing one another's cultures. But there was also war, over everything from personal squabbles between leaders, to fights over land, to misunderstandings and hatreds between different religions.

In England the royal family was fighting its own private war. Far to the north in Scandinavia, literature and history writing flourished as Icelanders began to write the sagas of their daring Viking ancestors. And in southern Spain three religions created a vibrant culture, until religious wars threatened to tear it apart.

WHEN THEY RULED
England—The Plantagenet Dynasty
1154—1485

Scandinavia   The Medieval Period
1066—1389

Spain—The Muslim Period
710—1492

THE ENGLISH
A FAMILY FEUD SHAPES HISTORY

The year 1200 in Europe was the high point of the Middle Ages, the period from about 500 to 1500. People often think of life back then as a fairy-tale world, full of kings, castles, knights in shining armor, and ladies in tall pointy hats.

The reality was different. Most people didn't live in castles and couldn't afford armor. The pointy hats were only in fashion for a few decades. Even the kings didn't have fairy-tale lives. For example, look at King Henry II of England and his wife, Queen Eleanor. These days we'd call them a dysfunctional family. In their own time people said they were descended from the Devil.

Henry ruled England and more than half of what is now France. His great-grandfather William I had been the Duke of Normandy in France before conquering England and making himself its king in the year 1066. The family kept its lands in France, and Henry II gained more French territory when he married Eleanor. She was the countess of the rich French province of Aquitaine.

Henry and Eleanor had a long marriage and a large family. They founded a line of kings,

known as the Plantagenet dynasty, that lasted nearly 250 years. Their marriage, however, was not always peaceful. They fought a lot, often leading armies against each other. When Henry defeated Eleanor in 1173, he had her locked up in Salisbury Castle. She was only set free sixteen years later, when Henry died.

Henry and Eleanor had four sons: Henry, Richard, Geoffrey, and John. Today two of them are still famous. People think of King Richard the Lion-Hearted as a great hero, and John gets remembered as wicked King John, the enemy of Robin Hood.

When the boys were growing up, the writers of their time said other things about them. A monk named Gerald of Wales wrote that all four of them were handsome and smart but couldn't stay out of trouble. Young Henry was popular with everyone, but people said he spent too much time partying instead of learning how to

After decades of fighting each other, King Henry II and his wife Eleanor of Aquitaine were buried side by side at Fontevraut Abbey in France. Today these beautifully carved and painted tombs are empty. When the abbey was raided during the French Revolution, six hundred years after Henry and Eleanor's time, the royal tombs were broken open and the bones were thrown away.

rule. Richard was a famous poet and one of the most skillful warriors in the kingdom, but some people worried that fighting was all he cared about. Geoffrey was fun and probably the smartest of the four, but he loved to talk people into fighting, just to see what would happen. John had the bad luck

This romantic picture of King Richard the Lion-Hearted feasting with Robin Hood and his merry men was painted centuries after the king's death. It may not tell us much about what life was like for real kings and outlaws in the twelfth century, but it says a lot about Richard's lasting popularity as a warrior king.

DEVIL'S BROOD

King Henry's sons had always known the legend that their family was related to the Devil. They laughed about it and used it as an excuse when people complained that they fought too much.

The story went that one of King Henry's ancestors had been married to a beautiful woman named Melusine. He loved her very much but couldn't help noticing that she was always absent from church when Communion was given. One day he made her stay. As the church service began, she screamed, flew out the window, and was never seen again. It turned out that Melusine was the daughter of the Devil. But by then she and her husband had two sons, half human and half demon. So Henry, Richard, Geoffrey, and John could say that they came by their devilishness naturally.

Their parents probably got very sick of that excuse!

When this sculpture from Notre Dame Cathedral in Paris was carved, Henry and Eleanor's three elder sons were around eight, six, and five years old. Every time they went to church they saw images like this of devils and angels weighing human souls.

*For medieval Christians, joining a crusade to conquer the
Holy Land was a way of earning forgiveness for their sins. In this
picture, King Richard and his army are on their way to Jerusalem.
Women often went on crusades with their husbands, like the
lady shown here riding in a palanquin on top of a camel.*

to be the youngest, so he always had to live up to his famous brothers.
   In 1173, when they were eighteen, sixteen, and fifteen, Henry, Richard,
and Geoffrey sided with Eleanor and went to war against their father.
They lost, and their mother was imprisoned, but the boys and the king

made up. John was only five but got his share of family fights later.

A knight once asked Geoffrey why he and his family were always fighting. Geoffrey said, "It's our inheritance from long ago that none of us loves the others, and we always have to do our best to hurt each other." Sometimes, though, they did seem to care about one another. Once, when young Henry and Geoffrey had joined forces against Richard and King Henry, the king was almost killed by one of Prince Henry's archers. The prince immediately called off the fighting and ran to apologize to his father and make sure he was all right.

King Henry's sons might have been dangerous, but people loved them. When Prince Henry died of dysentery at age twenty-eight, a knight named William Marshal vowed to go on a Crusade to Jerusalem in the prince's name, hoping that would save Prince Henry's soul. Geoffrey was killed three years later in a tournament accident, when he was knocked off his horse and trampled to death. At his funeral his friend King Philip II of France was so upset he tried to jump into Geoffrey's grave.

Today when families fight and children rebel against their parents, they don't usually have armies backing them up. Historical writers of King Henry's time, like the monk Gerald of Wales, believed that only the Devil could cause so much trouble in one family. But as Queen Eleanor says in *The Lion in Winter,* a play about Henry II's family written eight hundred years later, "What family doesn't have its ups and downs?"

THE SCANDINAVIANS
FROM PIRATES TO HISTORIANS

Nearly everyone has heard of the Vikings: pirates from Scandinavia who traveled in fast, dragon-headed longships and became famous as some of the best fighters and sailors of the Middle Ages. For years they terrorized Europe. Some even explored the North Atlantic Ocean as far as the Americas. They were so successful that the period from the late 700s to around 1100 is known as the Viking Age.

Not all Scandinavians were pirates. Many were farmers, fishermen, and merchants. But in Scandinavia (the area that today includes Denmark, Sweden, and Norway) there was a population increase in the eighth century, and there was not enough good farmland to feed all the people. In addition, new shipbuilding techniques allowed the sailors to go faster and farther than ever before. A lot of Scandinavian men, hearing merchants' tales about the riches they saw in foreign places, decided to seek their fortunes by plundering their neighbors. At first they only raided countries such as England, Ireland, and France. Later they set up trading centers there, and eventually many settled down, becoming farmers. A few Viking warriors became kings of the lands they conquered.

In Viking times storytelling was as important a skill as fighting. It wasn't any good being a great warrior if nobody heard about your heroic exploits. Poets called skalds, who recited the deeds of great kings and fighters, were some of the most respected people in Viking society. Best of all was to be a warrior *and* a skald, like Egil Skallagrimsson. This famous Viking once saved his own life by inventing a poem that flattered the king who was about to kill him.

By 1200 the time of the Vikings was over. Scandinavians were more interested in developing their own lands than conquering others.

This picture of Scandinavian warriors listening to a skald was created centuries after the Middle Ages. The simple helmets on four of the warriors give a good idea of the helmets worn by actual Vikings, but golden, winged helmets probably never existed outside of artists' imaginations.

Yet the exploits of the daring pirates continued to capture people's imaginations. The Scandinavians had mixed feelings about this. They didn't want the rest of Europe to think that they were still pirates, but they loved to tell the stories of their Viking ancestors.

The Vikings didn't write down their stories, but the Scandinavians who lived after them did. Writing about history was especially important in Iceland, an island that had been settled by Vikings from Norway. The Icelanders were proud of their brave and independent Norwegian ancestors. Writing and sharing the tales of Icelandic history helped the Icelanders remember why they should value their freedom. They also believed their history would make other people respect them. As one Icelander wrote around 1170, "People often say writing about history is irrelevant learning, but we think we can better meet the criticism of foreigners when they accuse us of being descended from slaves and

These farmhouses at the Skogar Folk Museum in Iceland, built of earth and stone, are similar to the houses medieval Icelanders would have known. When the Vikings first settled in Iceland there were trees on the island, but after a few centuries they had cut down too many of the trees for building houses and ships. The trees couldn't grow back fast enough, and the Icelanders had to find other building materials.

Elaborate wooden churches like this one in Norway were built around the time that the Scandinavians first became Christians.

scoundrels, if we know the truth about our ancestry. Anyway, all civilized peoples want to know about the origins of their own society."

The most famous of all Icelandic writers was Snorri Sturluson (SNORE-ree STOOR-loo-sawn), who was descended from the great Viking poet Egil. Snorri grew up surrounded by books. He was brought up by his foster father, his neighbor Jon Loftsson, whose grand estate was a center of learning and scholarship. When Snorri wrote his own histories of Scandinavia, he based them on the knowledge he'd gotten from the history and poetry books in Jon Loftsson's library.

Snorri became famous for his writing around 1215, when he composed a poem in honor of a powerful Norwegian nobleman. He traveled to Norway in 1218 to write poems for King Haakon (HAW-ken) IV and to research a book he was planning, a history of the kings of Norway. This book, the *Heimskringla*, is still one of the most famous works of medieval literature, and it's our most detailed source of knowledge about medieval Scandinavian history. Snorri wrote other books, including a saga about his famous

SNORRI'S BATH

Nowadays we often think of medieval people as being dirty and smelly and taking a bath once a year. While this sort of description is probably true of some medieval Europeans, the Scandinavians loved a good hot bath. At Reykjaholt, Snorri Sturluson's estate, tourists still visit the famous outdoor bath the poet had built.

Snorri never had to boil water for his bath. The water came from an underground hot spring. A partly covered stone drain led from the spring to a round bath, about four yards around and one yard deep, lined with flat, rectangular stone blocks. Here Snorri soaked in the naturally hot water while discussing politics and history with his friends or planning his next book.

ancestor Egil and a book called the *Prose Edda*, which preserves many legends from Scandinavian mythology. These stories, about the adventures of Norse gods such as Odin and Thor, would have been forgotten if Snorri hadn't written them down.

Unfortunately for Snorri, he wasn't a warrior like his ancestor Egil the Viking. Different branches of Snorri's family began fighting over whether Iceland should stay independent or be ruled by Norway. Though he had been a friend of Norway's King Haakon, Snorri supported Icelandic independence. In 1241 he was murdered on the orders of his son-in-law, who hoped to gain power in Iceland by throwing in his lot with Haakon.

Some kinds of power, however, don't last. Today barely anyone has heard of Gizur Thorvaldsson, Snorri's son-in-law. But the books of Snorri Sturlasson are still read around the world.

This modern statue shows a famous event in the life of King Haakon IV, when he was rescued as a baby from a rival king who wanted him killed. Today an annual ski race re-enacts the baby Haakon's trip over the snow-covered mountains. Each contestant in the race has to carry a backpack the same weight as a baby.

THE SPANISH
A SHAKY PEACE FALLS APART

Around 1200 there were two Spains. Northern Spain was Christian territory, made up of kingdoms such as León and Castile. The southern city-states such as Córdoba and Granada were Muslim.

The Muslims were Arabs, and they had lived in southern Spain, which they called al-Andalus, for nearly five hundred years. Muslims and Christians were often enemies, since the leaders of both religions claimed they had the only right ideas about God. But during the centuries that the two Spains existed, a lot of people from both faiths decided to try to work together.

This was partly because of Islamic ideas. The prophet Muhammad, who started Islam, is supposed to have said that people should "seek for knowledge even in China," meaning that learning was important no matter how far you had to go to get it. An educated person was respected. If you were a wise scholar or a skilled doctor, it didn't matter whether you were Muslim, Christian, or Jewish.

Muslims also had a tradition of respecting people of the Christian and Jewish faiths. They were, like the Muslims themselves, "people of the Book," meaning the Bible and the Koran. Each of the three religions taught that there was one all-powerful God, and many of the stories in their religious writings came from the same sources. In al-Andalus non-Muslims had to pay a special tax, and they weren't allowed to own Muslim slaves, but otherwise they were usually left to live as they wanted. Many Christians and Jews rose to powerful positions in the Andalusian government. It was a big contrast to most Christian European countries, where non-Christians seldom had political power.

By our 1200 date, though, this peace among the religions was falling apart. A group of Muslims from North Africa, the Almohads, had taken

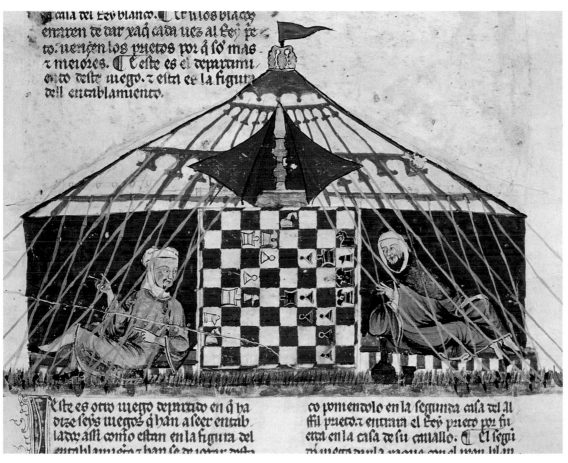

For those who were open-minded enough to learn from other cultures, the Muslim period in Spain was an exciting one. The Muslims introduced important new developments in science, art, literature, and even in the games people played. This medieval illustration shows two Arabs playing chess, a game they are believed to have introduced to Europe.

over the government in al-Andalus. They had strict ideas about how to treat non-Muslims, and they tried to force the Spanish Jews and Christians to convert to Islam. Many who refused were killed, while others fled the country.

Even the Spanish Muslims weren't happy with their new rulers. They

WISE KINGS

Though differences in religious beliefs caused much conflict on the Spanish peninsula, there were people who tried to make things better. Two Christian kings in particular, both named Alfonso, were known for being tolerant and open-minded.

When King Alfonso VI captured the Islamic city of Toledo in 1085, he kept Arabic as the official language. The king filled his court with Muslims and Jews as well as Christians. There were so many Jews in his army that he agreed not to make them fight on Saturday, the Jewish Sabbath.

A later Alfonso, King Alfonso X, who ruled from 1252 to 1284, was known as El Sabio, or "the Wise." He spoke Arabic as easily as Spanish and worked with Christian, Muslim, and Jewish scholars to translate books of science and philosophy as well as stories and poetry. So that more people could read the books, he translated them into the everyday languages people spoke, not the Latin that was used in the Christian church. One of his friends was a Muslim philosopher named al-Riqiti. King Alfonso built al-Riqiti a school where students of all three religions could study together.

didn't complain too loudly, because the Almohads had armies to back them up. But so many Spanish Muslims disliked their new government that when the Christians from northern Spain attacked, the Almohad rulers didn't get much support from their subjects. Partly because of this, in the 1200s the Christian kings conquered most of Spain. By the end of the fifteenth century, they would control the whole Spanish peninsula and drive out the Muslims and Jews.

Moses ben Maimon—often known by the Latin version of his name, Maimonides (my-MAH-nuh-deez)—was one Spaniard whose life was shaped

This page from one of El Sabio's books shows a royal court scene, probably based on life in El Sabio's own palace. Here a king and queen and some of their nobles listen to a musician.

by both the open-mindedness of Andalusian culture and the persecutions of the Almohads.

Maimonides was born around 1135 in Córdoba, an important city in al-Andalus. His father, Maimon, was a famous Jewish scholar and rabbi. Maimon wanted his son to be a scholar as well, but Maimonides wasn't interested in studying. The more his father yelled at him for not studying, the more Maimonides ignored him, which of course only made things worse.

It finally got so bad that Maimonides ran away from home. All of Rabbi

Maimon's attempts to find him failed, and finally the family gave up hope. Then one day Maimon went to the synagogue to hear a lecture by a visiting scholar. The scholar, who the audience agreed was one of the wisest young men they'd ever heard, was Maimonides. He'd learned on his own what his father hadn't been able to make him learn.

Around that time the Almohads conquered Córdoba. Rather than give up their religion, Maimonides and his family escaped to other cities in the Islamic world. They'd live in one city for a few years, then the government there would become harsher on non-Muslims and they'd have to leave again.

The island fortress of Majorca falls to the Christians in 1229. This wall painting was made by an unknown Muslim artist in the Middle Ages.

Spanish Jews, around 1350, worship in a synagogue similar to the synagogues where Maimonides studied and taught before the Almohad takeover.

While on the run from the Almohads, Maimonides became friends with Ibn-Rushd (ih-bun-ROOSHT), another scholar from Córdoba. Though Ibn-Rushd was Muslim, his ideas were too liberal for the Almohads, and Maimonides had to help him escape.

Despite the hardships, Maimonides continued his studies. He became an expert on Jewish legal and religious writings and also a skilled doctor. His wanderings ended in Egypt, where he became the chief physician to the Islamic ruler. Later Maimonides worked for Saladin (SA-luh-deen), the most famous Islamic leader in the Crusades, and wrote a medical textbook for Saladin's son. Though he spent nearly fifty years in Egypt, Maimonides always thought of al Andalus as his home. In his writings he called himself "the son of Rabbi Maimon the Spaniard."

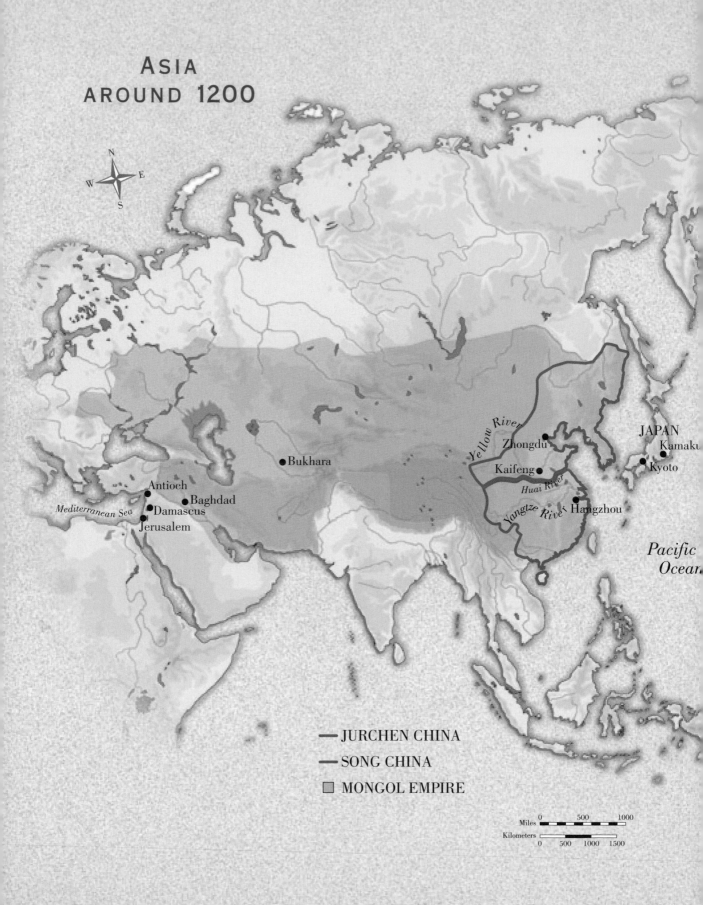

ASIA
AROUND 1200

N
W · E
S

JAPAN
Kamaku
Kyoto

Yellow River
Zhongdu
Kaifeng
Huai River
Yangtze River Hangzhou

Bukhara

Antioch
Baghdad
Mediterranean Sea
Damascus
Jerusalem

Pacific
Ocean

JURCHEN CHINA
SONG CHINA
MONGOL EMPIRE

Miles   0   500   1000
Kilometers
        0   500   1000   1500

PART II

ASIA

People often talk about Europe and Asia as if they are two different worlds. But in these worlds there have always been similarities. Around 1200 Asia, like Europe, was torn by religious wars and competing empires. As in Europe, people were developing new systems of government and creating works of art that would have a lasting impact on the world. At the western edge of Asia, in Palestine, Muslims and Christians were fighting over a country both believed to be holy. To the east, in a land of grass-covered plains most Europeans had never heard of, a young man was building a warrior nation that would dominate the Eurasian continent. In the Far East an ancient civilization was reaching new heights of art and science. And in an island country off the eastern coast of the continent, two brothers were creating a new form of government that would survive for more than six hundred years.

WHEN THEY RULED

The Crusades
1095—1291

The Mongol Empire
1183—1368

China—The Southern Song Dynasty
1127—1279

Japan—The Medieval Period
1185—1603

SARACENS AND CRUSADERS
FIGHTING FOR GOD

Saladin, sultan of Egypt, was out riding with his friend Baha al-Din. The sultan had a distant look on his face, and Baha al-Din asked what he was thinking.

"I think," said Saladin, "when Allah grants me victory over these crusaders I'll divide my territories, write my will, set sail for the lands of the Christians, and fight them in their own countries. I'll free the world from these people who don't believe in Allah, or I'll die trying."

His friend stared. "But you're the guardian of Islam," he protested. "You shouldn't risk your life on some rickety little ship!"

Saladin smiled. "What's the best possible death?"

"Death in the service of Allah," said Baha al-Din.

"So the worst that can happen to me is the best possible death. Why should I be afraid?"

When Baha al-Din wrote down that conversation, Saladin was the most powerful Muslim leader in the region of western Asia we call the Middle East. For all of Saladin's life, there had been conflict between his people and the European Christian warriors known as the crusaders. The First Crusade began about forty years before Saladin was born, and the last, the Eighth Crusade, ended in 1291, ninety-eight years after Saladin's death.

The focus of this fighting was Jerusalem, a holy city to all the "people of the Book." The Jews thought of Jerusalem as their ancient capital.

The artist who painted this fourteenth-century French picture of Saladin's army probably never saw a Saracen. The warriors in the picture look almost the same as European knights, but to make them look more foreign, the artist has given them turbans.

Their great king David had ruled there, and it was the site of their most important temple. The Muslims had an important mosque in Jerusalem, the Dome of the Rock, and they believed that Jerusalem was where all humans would be judged when the world came to an end. For Christians, Jerusalem was where Jesus was crucified and buried, and where

Christianity began. Everyone wanted to control Jerusalem, and the Holy City and the lands around it became a battlefield.

Muslims had ruled Jerusalem since 637. But during the First Crusade, in July 1095, a Christian army led by western European nobles and princes captured the city. So many of Jerusalem's inhabitants were killed that the crusaders' horses splashed in puddles of blood as they rode through the streets.

Religion was one of many motives for the Crusades. Many leading

The Dome of the Rock mosque in Jerusalem is built on the site where the prophet Muhammad is said to have ascended into heaven to receive the teachings of Allah. The mosque today remains much the same as when it was built, 1,300 years ago.

THE LEPER KING

The Saracens weren't the only ones who had great leaders.

Baldwin IV became king of the Christian Kingdom of Jerusalem in 1174, at age thirteen. His father, King Amalric, chose Baldwin as the next king because he was the smartest, kindest, and bravest of the candidates for the throne and had the best chance of holding the kingdom together. Saladin was already building up his power, and the leading crusader nobles were starting to fight among themselves. But they believed that with Baldwin as king, they still had a chance for victory.

This proves how much they admired Baldwin, because by the time he was thirteen he was already dying. At age nine he'd started showing signs of leprosy, one of the most feared diseases of the Middle Ages. By the time Baldwin died, when he was twenty-four, the disease had eaten away his feet, hands, and face until he was unrecognizable. Near the end he had to be carried into battle, because his body was too weak for him to ride on his own.

Even so, Baldwin led his armies to major victories against Saladin. Like the people of Jerusalem, Saladin admired the dying king. Once Saladin was besieging a crusader castle and looked certain to win. King Baldwin led a relief expedition, and Saladin respected his fellow monarch so much that he ended the siege before the two armies even met. One of the few men to ever defeat Saladin was a teenager who was too ill to walk.

crusaders had joined the fight because they didn't have land of their own at home, and they hoped to keep for themselves whatever cities they captured in the Holy Land. For a few of them, it worked. The new Christian Kingdom of Jerusalem was ruled by a king elected from among the crusading princes. Other captured cities, such as Antioch, became

Saladin was famous even among his enemies. This portrait of the great leader was painted in Italy centuries after his death.

semi-independent regions ruled by powerful crusaders.

The crusaders believed that God had given the Holy Land back to them. But the Muslims—whom the Christians called Saracens, from an ancient Greek name for Arab nomads—weren't giving up so easily.

One reason the First Crusade had succeeded was that there was no strong Muslim government in the Middle East. The empire of the Seljuk Turks, which controlled the area for much of the eleventh century, was collapsing. The soldiers of the First Crusade had faced many small countries, which were also fighting against one another, instead of one unified force.

Having the crusader kingdoms as a common enemy helped convince Middle Eastern Muslims that they should join forces. By the twelfth century the crusaders in the Holy Land had to ask for help from Europe to fight three powerful Muslim rulers: Zengi, his son Nur al-Din, and, most famous of all the Saracens, Nur al-Din's general, Saladin.

Not much is known about Saladin's early life, but one story says that while fighting in the Saracen army as a boy, he was captured and made a slave by crusaders. He seems to have been well liked by his Christian masters, and his main duty was to baby-sit Stephanie, daughter of a crusading noble. Saladin either escaped or was ransomed by his family, and he rose through the ranks in Nur al-Din's army.

The story of Saladin as a slave has come to us from only one source, and we don't know if it's true. But if it is, it could help explain Saladin's later encounters with his enemies. Among the crusaders and back in Europe, Saladin was famous for his kindness. He had friendly conversations with Christian knights he captured, and once when he heard that an enemy leader was sick with a fever, he sent presents of fruit and snow. Another time, when the wives of some captured Christians begged Saladin to free their husbands, he let the men go without asking for one penny of ransom. But though he often liked them, Saladin believed it was his duty to fight the crusaders. They were the enemies of Allah, so they were Saladin's enemies too.

Saladin was so famous in Europe that when King Henry II of England raised a tax to help pay for the Crusades, it was called the "Saladin tax." In 1187 Saladin's army captured Jerusalem, ending nearly a century of Christian rule. The war dragged on for another hundred years, but the crusaders never regained lasting control of Jerusalem.

Many years later, an Italian named Dante wrote a famous poem in which he described an imaginary trip through heaven and hell. He showed what he thought about people from history by describing their punishments in hell or their rewards in heaven. Dante wrote that Muhammad, the founder of Islam, was in hell suffering horrible tortures. But Saladin, even though he fought and defeated the Christians, wasn't in hell. He was somewhere between hell and heaven. Long after the Crusades were over, Saladin's reputation in the Christian countries was as mixed as it had been with the crusaders. He was the enemy, but he was also capable of great kindness and noble deeds.

THE MONGOLS
WARRIORS ON HORSEBACK BUILD AN EMPIRE

"I am the punishment of God," Genghis Khan declared. "If you had not committed great sins, he would not have sent a punishment like me."

A Persian historian reported that Genghis Khan spoke these words in 1220 when he captured Bukhara, a rich and famous city in western Asia. Genghis Khan may not really have believed that he was God's vengeance, but he knew his enemies would believe it. Across Asia and Europe, Genghis and his Mongol warriors were feared. People who knew nothing about the Mongols said they were man-eating monsters with the heads of dogs. Suddenly, it seemed, their swift-moving armies mounted on horseback were conquering much of Asia and Europe.

Of course these fierce warriors hadn't come from nowhere. The Mongols were nomads who lived in central Asia, north of China. They raised herds of sheep, goats, cattle, and horses. In summer they lived on huge open plains with plenty of grazing. But the winters were harsh, so during the cold months the Mongols would move their families and herds into sheltered mountain valleys.

To keep moving, the Mongols needed good horses. Mongol children learned to ride almost before they could walk. Boys were taught to shoot arrows from horseback, so they could hunt wolves and deer and protect their families.

Around the middle of the twelfth century, few people in the West knew about the Mongols. They certainly weren't as famous as their neighbors the Chinese, with their cities and temples and palaces.

But Genghis Khan changed that.

Genghis Khan isn't a name. It's a title meaning "limitless ruler." As

Mongol men were trained in horsemanship from their earliest childhood. The Mongol warriors had to be able to fight and fire arrows from horseback, and they terrified enemy warriors who were used to fighting on foot.

a boy, Genghis was called Temujin. His father was murdered by an enemy tribe when Temujin was ten, and Temujin had to help his mother raise his younger brothers and sister.

The family's enemies tried to kill Temujin too, but he escaped and began gathering followers. People said his eyes were made of fire and his face was filled with light. No matter what the odds were against him, he managed to win. Soon it was a lot safer to be his friend than his enemy, and Temujin was good at rewarding the people who fought for him.

This portrait shows Genghis Khan in his old age, when he had transformed his people from an obscure tribe to the rulers of half a continent.

SECRET HISTORY

Before Genghis Khan, the Mongols didn't have a written language. Genghis decided that they would use the writing system of the Uighurs, a neighboring tribe. The khan who ruled after Genghis ordered his scholars to write a history of the Mongols, so no one would forget what a great leader Genghis had been. The book was called *The Secret History of the Mongols*, because only Mongols were supposed to read it.

The Secret History tells many stories of Temujin's early adventures. Once, it says, he was captured by some members of the tribe that had killed his father. They locked a huge wooden collar around his neck, but that didn't stop him. He knocked out his guard with the collar, ran away, and jumped into a lake. Through the night, while his enemies searched the land, he stayed in the lake with only his head above water. The collar kept him afloat.

Another time, all but one of the family horses were stolen. Temujin set out on the last horse to get the others back. Along the way he met a boy his own age who'd seen which way the horse thieves had gone. The boy, Borchu, offered to help Temujin, and together they stole back the horses. Borchu and Temujin remained friends all their lives, and Borchu became one of Genghis Khan's greatest generals.

In 1206 he was proclaimed Genghis Khan, ruler of all the Mongols. Genghis set about organizing a huge army. Every man older than fourteen was called into service. Each recruit was required to come to the ruler's camp, bringing four or five horses with him. Mongol warriors could live for weeks off a mixture of fermented mare's milk and blood drawn from the

MOBILE HOMES

Some things haven't changed in eight hundred years. The Mongols of Genghis Khan's time lived in the same kind of houses that most Mongols do today.

Mongols call these houses *ger,* meaning "home," although in English we often use the word *yurt.* A *ger* has a round wooden frame of several interlocking sections tied together. The frame is covered with felt, made by beating and rolling wet wool. One of the titles given to Genghis Khan was "ruler of all the people who live in felt tents."

A *ger* may not sound fancy, but it's warm in winter, and in summer the felt walls can be rolled up. Most important, it can be set up in a half hour, taken down in fifteen minutes, and is easy to carry on carts, so the Mongol armies could take their houses with them. Genghis Khan, though, didn't have to take down his ger. His soldiers just loaded it, fully set up, onto a giant cart pulled by oxen.

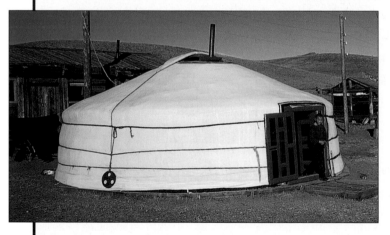

Genghis was probably the only king around 1200 who had a palace on wheels.

The ger is a common sight in Mongolia today, just as it was eight hundred years ago.

horses. This brew, which provided iron and protein, was carried in leather canteens. Other armies often got beaten when they couldn't get food supplies from home, but the Mongols, who also brought along their families and herds, had everything they needed. And since they were superb horsemen, they could move faster than their enemies.

With their new army the Mongols trampled all opposition. Any city that tried to resist them was laid waste, with most of its people slaughtered. Leaving a path lined with mountains of skulls, the Mongols built the largest empire in the world. By the time Genghis Khan died, in 1227, they had conquered territory as far west as Bulgaria and as far east as northern China. In 1279, under Genghis's grandson Kublai Khan, they conquered all of China, where they would rule for nearly a hundred years.

Although people had good reason to fear the Mongols, being ruled by them wasn't such a bad thing. The Mongols allowed the people they conquered to run their countries the way they had before, as long as they paid tribute to the khan and let him make their foreign policies. The Mongols didn't try to force other people to live the way they did, unlike the rulers of many other empires. People were allowed to keep their own religions, and Genghis liked to talk with the priests of conquered countries. He was polite to them, but he wasn't convinced that any one religion was right. Genghis said that God didn't live in just one church or temple or mosque, but in the entire world.

Horses and horsemanship are still a crucial part of the Mongols' culture, and mare's milk is part of their everyday diet.

THE CHINESE
AT THE "CENTER" OF THE WORLD

In the nineteenth century the famous novelist Charles Dickens began one of his books with the words, "It was the best of times, it was the worst of times." Dickens was writing about France in the late 1700s, but those words could just as easily have applied to China around 1200.

Like people in many other countries, the Chinese in 1200 believed they had the most civilized country in the world. They called China the "Middle Kingdom," meaning that it was at the center of the world, and the rest of the world was barbaric in comparison.

China in 1200 does indeed seem more "modern" to us than other places in the world at that time. It had large, sophisticated cities, with public parks, fire brigades, and street lights. The government paid for medical care for the people. While most cities in Europe around 1200 were small, Hangzhou

A bustling street in the Chinese city of Kaifeng. We see shop-keepers and customers, horses and camels, and a sedan chair used for carrying wealthy men and women.

This portrait of Chao K'uang-yin, the first emperor of the Song dynasty, was painted around 1280. By this time the Mongols had defeated the last Song resistance and had conquered all of China.

(hahn-joh), the Chinese capital, had more than a million inhabitants.

China was one of the world's first civilizations, dating back to around 3000 B.C. In 1200 the land was ruled by an emperor of the Song (or Sung) dynasty. The Song period (960–1279) is often spoken of as a high point in Chinese culture. Chinese merchant ships sailed to countries all over southern and western Asia, and as far away as Africa. The sailors on these ships navigated using magnetic compasses, which were invented in Song China. Agriculture was prospering, thanks largely to the introduction of a type of rice that gave two crops a year. Huge advances were being made in medicine, such as the development of an inoculation against smallpox. The landscape paintings created in this period are said to be the greatest in the history of Chinese art. Also in the Song period, China started

Government jobs in medieval China were filled by scholars, who were chosen for their jobs through exams that required huge amounts of memorization. The scholars shown in this Song dynasty painting were among the most powerful men in Chinese society. But they didn't have the skills and experience to fight nomadic warrior cultures like the Jurchen and the Mongols.

exporting large amounts of fine porcelain to countries all over the world. For centuries only the Chinese knew how to make this porcelain. Not until the 1700s did German potters figure out the secret of making "china."

Despite all these advances, in 1200 China was in trouble. In fact, many of the advances happened *because* of the trouble.

In 1200 the Chinese emperor ruled only half the territory that previous emperors had ruled a century before. Northern China had been conquered in 1126 by a tribe of nomadic warriors called the Jurchens, who were neighbors and rivals of the Mongols. The Jurchens captured the old capital city, Kaifeng, and made prisoners of the Song emperor Qinzong and most of his family. By the time Qinzong died in captivity, the Jurchens had already set up their own government in the northern city of Zhongdu (modern-day Beijing). They ruled all of China north of the Huai River until 1234, when it was their turn to be defeated, by the Mongols.

Prince Gaozong, a younger brother of the captured emperor, escaped and set up a southern Chinese government in Hangzhou. He faced another fifteen years of war before making peace with the Jurchens, but Gaozong became the first emperor of the Southern Song dynasty.

Defeat hurt Chinese pride. But in many ways, losing the north was good for China's economy. The Song still controlled the richest farmlands, which were all in the south. Since they no longer had access to most of the overland trade routes, they had to focus on overseas trade instead. In previous centuries the Arabs had controlled oceangoing trade along the coasts of Africa and Asia, but in the Southern Song period the Chinese came to dominate these trade routes. The number of men in the Chinese navy went from about 3,000 in the year 1130 to nearly 52,000 in 1237. Their ships, first designed for traveling on the Chinese rivers, had watertight compartments in their holds, which meant they could stay afloat after they'd sprung a leak.

The Chinese, who'd invented gunpowder during the Tang dynasty (A.D. 618–907), were also the first people in the world to use gunpowder in war. The technique for making explosives was first described in a Chinese

EMPRESS MENG
SAVES THE DYNASTY

It was a difficult job, choosing an empress. Meng, the sixteen-year-old daughter of an important army officer, was chosen from one hundred candidates to become the chief wife, or empress, of Emperor Zhezong (ruled 1085 to 1105). Unfortunately, Zhezong's mother picked Meng for him. To prove that he wasn't ruled by his mother, he paid more attention to another of his wives, named Liu. Liu wanted so badly to be the empress that she accused Meng of witchcraft.

Meng was found guilty and sent to live in a religious sanctuary, while Liu became the new empress. That should have been the end of the story. Instead, Meng was one of the few members of the imperial family to escape when the Jurchens captured northern China years later.

Even though she was still in the north, under Jurchen control, Meng publicly supported Prince Gaozong's claim to be the new Chinese emperor. Gaozong helped her escape from northern China, and she became an influential leader in Gaozong's new government in the south. Having the support of a former empress made Gaozong a lot easier to accept as emperor. In 1129 Meng took a more active role in supporting Gaozong. He'd been defeated in a battle with the Jurchens, and the captains of his bodyguard rebelled against him. They set up his three-year-old son as emperor in his place and asked Meng to rule until the boy came of age. Meng agreed, so she could protect the boy, but she was secretly in contact with Gaozong. When Gaozong gained control of the army again, Meng returned the throne to him and stayed on as one of the most respected figures of his court.

It wasn't the future she'd imagined when she was sixteen. But she'd played a more important role in Chinese history than most empresses—and most emperors.

The Song emperors founded a royal academy of painting, and Song dynasty painting styles were influenced by the tastes of the royal family. Pictures of birds and flowers, as well as portraits of pets and children, were among the royal family's favorite styles of art.

military handbook from 1044. At first they used simple hand-thrown grenades, but things quickly got more complicated. Around 1150 Chinese soldiers started using arrow rocket launchers. They wrapped a gunpowder charge in oiled paper and strapped it to an arrow. The arrows were held in a cone-shaped wood or bamboo launcher. They could fly as far as 1,100 feet. The Chinese also used the first gun ever invented, which was simply a long bamboo tube from which bullets were fired when the gunpowder was lighted.

In their battles in the 1250s through the 1270s, the Chinese gave the Mongols a run for their money. But in 1279, the Song were defeated as much by their own government as by the Mongols. Earlier in the century the Song had joined forces with the Mongols when the nomadic warriors attacked Jurchen-ruled China. Perhaps Song leaders hoped that when the Mongols destroyed the Jurchens, the Song could regain control of northern China. Instead, they became the Mongols' next target.

THE JAPANESE
CLASH OF THE SAMURAI

The people of Kyoto, Japan, were terrified.

Kyoto was the capital, the emperor's own city. But the emperor's guards couldn't do anything about Benkei the warrior monk.

People said he was a ten-foot-tall demon. Actually he was only seven feet. And he wasn't a demon—he just liked proving he was the best fighter around. He'd vowed that he would duel with every warrior he met, and when he won, he would take their swords. He had 999 swords already.

The night he planned to take his 1,000th sword, Benkei saw a boy walking toward him, playing a bamboo flute. But what Benkei noticed was the boy's beautiful gold-handled sword.

"Hand over your sword, little boy," roared Benkei.

The boy stopped playing the flute and smiled. "Sorry," he said. "It's a family heirloom."

Benkei laughed and started swinging his big *naginata* spear.

Before Benkei knew it, the boy drew his sword. It gleamed in the moonlight, and Benkei's spear was sliced in half.

Benkei drew his own sword. But suddenly his weapon was on the ground, and the boy was picking it up, saying, "I ought to take this from you, but then you might think I need it." He handed it back.

"Who are you?" gasped Benkei.

"Minamoto Yoshitsune."

Benkei kneeled and bowed until his head touched the ground. "Let me follow you," he said.

"It won't be an easy path."

"I know, my lord," said Benkei. "That's why you'll need friends."

Countless legends have grown up around the hero Yoshitsune. In one story, he learned his fighting skills from tengu, fierce forest spirits with the heads of birds.

The famous legend of Benkei and Yoshitsune's meeting is probably more fairy tale than fact. But the two were real people, and they played crucial roles in Japanese history.

Yoshitsune was the youngest son of a warrior named Minamoto Yoshitomo. The Minamoto clan had been at war for years with another clan, the Taira.

When Yoshitsune was a baby, his father was killed. The leader of the Taira let Yoshitomo's children live, but on condition that none of the boys be trained as warriors. They had to be brought up in monasteries and become Buddhist monks.

At his monastery in the mountains, Yoshitsune trained in secret, sneaking out at night to practice swordplay and archery with an old man who lived in the forest. When he was fifteen years old, he ran away from the monastery to find his brothers. He hoped that they could defeat the Taira and avenge their father's death.

The Minamoto and Taira were both clans of samurai. *Samurai* means "servant," and samurai were supposed to serve the government. These warriors kept the peace and punished the government's enemies.

At the top of the government was the emperor, who was believed to be descended from the Sun Goddess. Working for him were the nobles, and the samurai worked for them.

But the noble families had been in power for so long that most of them had forgotten how to work. They lived in Kyoto and never traveled to the rest of the country. More and more of the real work was being done by people who

This battle scene shows samurai of the Minamoto army. Among the weapons they hold are swords, called "the souls of the samurai," bows and arrows, and a curved naginata spear.

MASAKO, THE NUN SHOGUN

In Japan around 1200, as in most other places across the globe, people thought that women weren't as important as men. Women were supposed to do what they were told to do by the men in their families. But there were always women who proved that they were as intelligent and brave as men.

When Minamoto Yoritomo's armies were hunting Yoshitsune, they captured Yoshitsune's girlfriend, Shizuka, and brought her to Yoritomo. Shizuka argued with Yoritomo and told him he would never be as great a leader as Yoshitsune. Yoritomo wanted to kill her, but his wife, Masako, convinced him to spare Shizuka's life.

After Yoritomo died, Masako became a Buddhist nun, as was expected of Japanese widows. But being a nun didn't stop Masako from becoming the most powerful person in the country. Her two sons each became shogun. Both, however, were murdered by enemies who wanted to capture the government. Masako crushed those takeover attempts and made her brother the ruler. The men in her family officially ruled Japan, but it was Masako who made the decisions. She was known as the Nun Shogun.

lived in the countryside, like the samurai. Some of them began to wonder why they should serve men who never did anything but sit in Kyoto and write poetry. Why couldn't the samurai run the government themselves?

In secret, Yoshitsune and his oldest brother, Yoritomo, started gathering warriors. They fought their first battle against the Taira in 1180, and lost. But by 1185 the Minamoto armies had destroyed the Taira, and Yoritomo

Minamoto Yoritomo, the first shogun, left his mark on centuries of Japanese history, but he's most often remembered as the jealous brother who hunted down Yoshitsune.

Like his friend and master Yoshitsune, Benkei has become a hero of legends and fairy tales. In one of the most famous adventures, set during Benkei's childhood, Benkei fights and kills a monster carp.

was the most powerful man in Japan.

Yoshitsune had been his brother's most successful general. He knew how to take his enemies by surprise. In one battle he had his men charge on horseback down a hill that was so steep even monkeys were afraid to descend it. His men thought they'd break their necks, but they made it down alive and won the battle, since the Taira had been waiting for them to attack from another direction.

Yoritomo built the government of his dreams. He became the first shogun, or military ruler, of Japan. Instead of ruling through the emperor and his nobles, Yoritomo set up a new government in a different town, Kamakura. He allowed the emperor to continue to live in Kyoto, but Kamakura was where all the decisions were made.

Yoritomo's system of government, in which the shogun was the true ruler and the emperor was just a figurehead, lasted more than six hundred years. But the Minamoto brothers didn't live very long after coming to power. Jealousy was mainly to blame.

Yoritomo had long been jealous of Yoshitsune. After becoming shogun, he feared his daring brother would try to take the government from him, just as he himself had taken power away from the emperor.

So he sent an army to attack Yoshitsune and his men.

Benkei, the warrior monk, was with Yoshitsune to the end. Benkei fought off the army long enough for Yoshitsune to kill himself, so no one could brag they had killed Japan's greatest general.

Ten years later, in 1199, Yoritomo too was dead, killed by a fall from his horse. Although Yoritomo had defeated the Taira and started the rule of the shogun, it is Yoshitsune and Benkei that the Japanese remember. Yoshitsune is still the most famous samurai in Japanese history. He was so popular in his time that when he died, people refused to believe he was dead. Instead they told a story that he had escaped to the Chinese mainland, taken a new identity, and become—Genghis Khan!

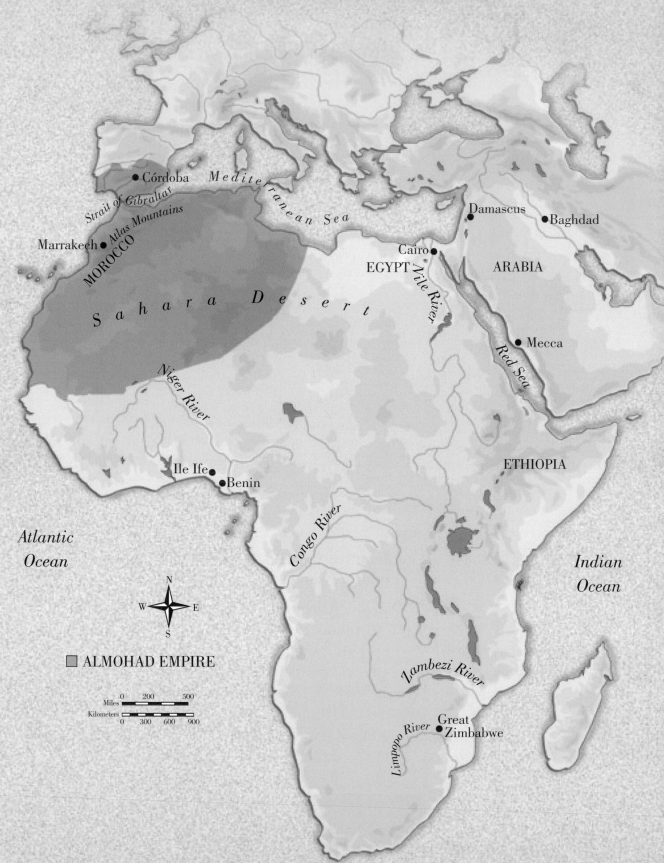

AFRICA AROUND 1200

Córdoba

Mediterranean Sea

Damascus

Baghdad

Strait of Gibraltar

Atlas Mountains

Marrakech

MOROCCO

Cairo

EGYPT

Nile River

ARABIA

Sahara   Desert

Red Sea

Mecca

Niger River

Ile Ife

Benin

ETHIOPIA

Atlantic
Ocean

Congo River

Indian
Ocean

N

W   E

S

■ ALMOHAD EMPIRE

Zambezi River

Miles   0   200   500

Kilometers   0   300   600   900

Limpopo River

Great
Zimbabwe

PART III

AFRICA

The African continent around the year 1200 was a varied and exciting place. The religion of Islam had been brought from Arabia five hundred years earlier, and the people of North Africa were now mostly Muslims. They had close political and cultural ties to the Middle East. North Africa was also very involved with the politics of Europe, and caravan routes across the Sahara Desert linked the north with thriving kingdoms in West Africa. Further south, remarkable stone cities were being built by people who grew wealthy herding cattle and trading gold. And in the northeastern corner of the continent, there were several kingdoms that many centuries earlier had adopted Christianity, another religion that had begun in the Middle East.

WHEN THEY RULED

The Almohad Empire
1130—1269

The Yoruba Kingdoms
around 1000—1800

Zimbabwe—The Age of the Great

Enclosures
around 1000—1500

Ethiopia—The Zagwe Dynasty
1137—1270

THE ALMOHADS
AN EMPIRE BASED ON FAITH

It wasn't very impressive, the little Berber village where the boy grew up in the mountains of Morocco. Stone houses huddled together amid scraggly trees, and people raised sparse crops and herded animals over the rocky hillsides. In this simple village Muhammad Ibn Tumart stood out. He was a bright boy, curious about everything. So they sent him to the local school.

He learned many things there, but not enough to answer all his questions. To learn more, young Ibn Tumart traveled to what were then some of the world's greatest places of learning—to Córdoba in Spain, Mecca in Arabia, Baghdad in present-day Iraq, and Cairo in Egypt. Asking questions everywhere, he gradually began forming answers of his own. Some people agreed with his ideas about religion and government, and as he moved from city to city in North Africa, they became his followers. When he returned to Morocco he stopped in the city of Marrakech. There he loudly objected to certain laws until the emir, the government leader, tried to have him jailed. Fleeing to his native mountains, Ibn Tumart began what was called the Almohad movement, meaning "people who believe in the oneness of God." Ibn Tumart was so loved by his followers that when he died, his close friends kept his death secret for years so that the Almohads would not lose heart. But eventually one of his followers was chosen leader, and after twenty years of warfare, the Almohads took over the government of North Africa.

By the year 1200 Ibn Tumart had been dead more than fifty years, but the Almohad Empire had become large and powerful. It included most of North Africa, West Africa as far south as the Niger River, and much of Spain.

The Almohad Empire was based not only on military power but also on the Islamic religion. Ibn Tumart's complaint about the earlier leaders was

The introduction of camels by the Arabs changed the whole way of life for people like Ibn Tumart's Berber tribe. The sturdy camels made it possible to travel long distances across the desert and opened up opportunities for travel and trade that had never existed before.

that they had made too many changes in Muhammad's teachings. Muhammad had begun the religion of Islam in 622 in Arabia, and after his death Arab armies had quickly spread the new religion through western Asia. The process took longer in North Africa because the native Berber tribes resisted Arab political control. Eventually, though, most did accept the new religion, and it gave them a new unity. Instead of fighting one another, the Berbers now fought other people and spread Islam.

Berbers made up most of the Arab-led armies that crossed the Strait of

This picture was painted in Baghdad in the year 1237. Slave markets like the one shown here were an everyday part of the Almohads' world. The fear on the face of the child in green suggests that the painter felt some sympathy for the slaves' situation.

Gibraltar and conquered southern Spain. Later, Almohad Berbers controlled the trade routes south across the Sahara Desert into the rest of Africa. Almohad traders exchanged their cloth, salt, and metal for ivory, gold, and slaves. This contact also spread the Islamic religion into West Africa. Since Islam did not permit making slaves of fellow believers, people were encouraged to adopt Islam as a way to protect themselves from slavery.

A half century after our 1200 date, the Almohad Empire broke apart. But North Africans remained a proud part of the Islamic world. That world was ahead of Europe in many areas—in art and music, in architecture and medicine, and in astronomy and mathematics. Islamic cities from Córdoba in Spain, to Cairo in Egypt, to Damascus and Baghdad in the Middle East flourished as centers of learning and trade. And thanks to Arab scholars, the knowledge of the ancient Western world, especially that of the Greeks, was preserved and passed on to Europe.

THE WILL OF GOD

Believers in Islam think that it is pointless to defy the will of Allah. This isn't fatalism—it doesn't mean that people shouldn't try to improve their lives. It means that people should be wise and seek to learn the will of Allah. In Almohad North Africa, where learning was treasured, many respected scholars lived in the cities while, in the mountains, "holy men" lived apart, striving to learn God's will.

This old Moroccan tale teaches about God's will and true wisdom:

In the wilderness there were evil spirits who delighted in causing trouble. Once an evil genie blocked an important mountain river with a huge rock. Soon the people nearby were dying of thirst, and their crops couldn't grow. They turned for help to the emir, who learned through holy magic that it was the will of God that the genie could be defeated only if forty wise men laid down their lives.

So the emir called together forty scholars and asked for their help. But they didn't want to die, and so they said that their wisdom wasn't strong enough because it came only from books. Then the emir called together forty holy men whose wisdom supposedly came directly from God. But they too feared to help. Finally another holy man, Sidi Rahal, came forward. Saying that he would defeat the genie by himself, he set out for the mountains.

Now the forty holy men were ashamed and said that they too would go to try to defeat the genie. When they reached the big rock that blocked the river, they sat below it where everyone could see them and began to pray.

Meanwhile, Sidi Rahal marched farther up the mountain. Alone in the wilderness, he recited holy incantations that so terrified the genie, the evil creature flew away. The river burst free, sending the rock soaring through the air. It landed on the forty wise men, killing them all.

Thus the will of Allah was fulfilled.

THE YORUBA
MASTERS OF CLAY AND BRONZE

Once there was only sky and sea. All the gods lived in the sky, but nothing much ever happened there. So Oduduwa, son of the chief god, was sent to climb down from heaven on a long iron chain. He carried with him a large snail shell full of dirt and a live chicken. When he was hanging just above the water, he dumped the dirt on its surface. Then he put down the chicken. As chickens do, it scratched and scratched, scattering dirt over the sea until solid land was created. Oduduwa then brought people down from the sky to live on the earth, and he became their first *oni*, or king.

This is the story the Yoruba people, who still live in the forests of western Nigeria, tell to explain how the world began. It is their creation myth. Their capital city, Ile Ife, takes its name from the myth. Ile Ife means "earth scattering," for the Yoruba believe it was the place where Oduduwa's chicken first scratched the dirt. Oduduwa's chain is said to be kept in a shrine there.

Archaeologists think that the Yoruba actually came from the grasslands to the northeast of Nigeria around the year 700. After they settled down, they mingled with the native Nok people, who were makers of animal and human figures in clay. The Yoruba took up this art, making beautiful clay heads of their own, and they also imported copper and other metals so they could make statues of bronze and brass. Today these "bronzes" are considered among the finest works of art in the world.

Around 1200 Ife was at its most prosperous. The city was surrounded by a tall earthen wall, and its streets were decoratively paved with white pebbles and pieces of broken pottery. Yoruba merchants plied their trade all over Africa, even crossing the hot and dry Sahara Desert. Most Yoruba were farmers, however, raising yams, other vegetables, and small livestock. Smaller Yoruba towns, sometimes also walled, were ruled by chiefs who were believed to be descended from the first people that Oduduwa brought to earth. But the *oni* of Ife was in the direct line of the first *oni*, Oduduwa himself, and so was considered almost a god.

To the Yoruba, gods were powerful and dangerous. The *oni* was seldom seen

The wooden masks created by modern Yoruba artists are strongly influenced by the bronze sculptures made by their ancestors. This is a Gelede mask, worn during a traditional dance to protect Yoruba villages from witchcraft. Masks like this are worn on the top of the head, and the dancer's face is covered by a cloth, like the veils that covered the faces of medieval Yoruba kings.

The vibrant red peppers in this market in modern Nigeria would have been unknown to the medieval Yoruba, since peppers are a plant originally grown in America. But in other ways, this crowded, lively market is probably very much like the Yoruba marketplaces of eight hundred years ago.

in public, and when he was, his face was veiled since it was thought his glance could kill. Most of the exquisite bronzes made in Ife were portraits of the *oni*. Many of these showed the ruler just from the neck up, since the Yoruba believed the head was the center of a person's power. The bronze statues the Yoruba created probably were placed on ancestral altars, where they could be honored by the living *oni*.

The Edo people, neighbors to the southeast, had similar customs to the Yoruba. Around 1200, when their king died without an heir, the elders of Benin, the Edo's capital city, sent to the *oni* of Ife and asked for one of his sons to be their ruler. The *oni* agreed, and the prince married a highborn Edo woman. Their son became the first *oba*, the

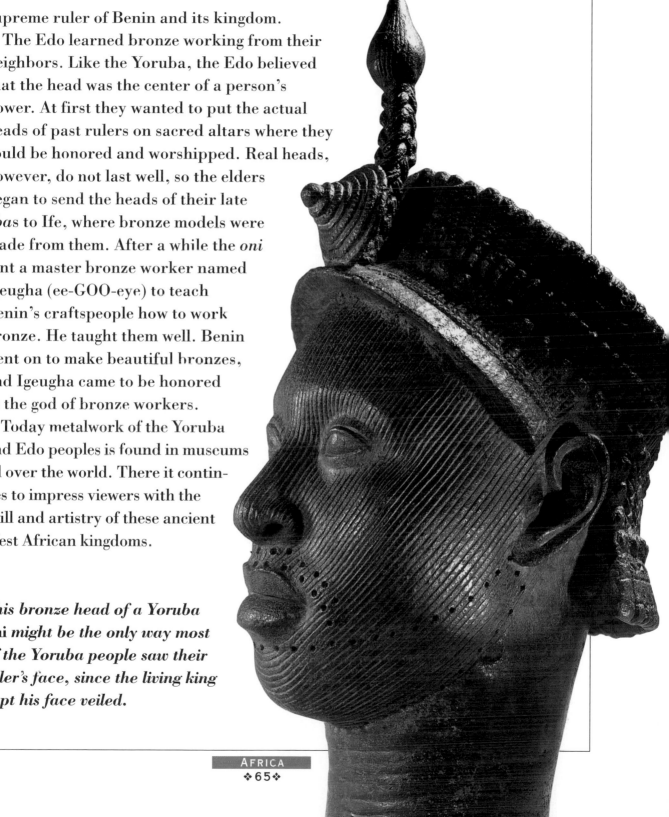

supreme ruler of Benin and its kingdom.

The Edo learned bronze working from their neighbors. Like the Yoruba, the Edo believed that the head was the center of a person's power. At first they wanted to put the actual heads of past rulers on sacred altars where they could be honored and worshipped. Real heads, however, do not last well, so the elders began to send the heads of their late *oba*s to Ife, where bronze models were made from them. After a while the *oni* sent a master bronze worker named Igeugha (ee-GOO-eye) to teach Benin's craftspeople how to work bronze. He taught them well. Benin went on to make beautiful bronzes, and Igeugha came to be honored as the god of bronze workers.

Today metalwork of the Yoruba and Edo peoples is found in museums all over the world. There it continues to impress viewers with the skill and artistry of these ancient West African kingdoms.

This bronze head of a Yoruba oni might be the only way most of the Yoruba people saw their ruler's face, since the living king kept his face veiled.

THE ZIMBABWEANS
THE LOST STONE BUILDERS

European explorers who stumbled across the ruins of Great Zimbabwe in the late 1800s thought at first that they had found King Solomon's ancient mines. On second thought, might this be the palace of the Queen of Sheba? Then again, perhaps the Phoenicians had sailed down the east coast of Africa, marched inland, and built this great stone city. It seemed impossible that such a grand city could possibly have been the work of Africans.

In fact, Africans started living in Great Zimbabwe, in southern Africa, about A.D. 500. By 1200 they had begun to construct buildings of stone. Great Zimbabwe eventually covered more than one hundred acres and was home to ten thousand people.

It was located in grassy plateau country in what is now the nation of Zimbabwe, which itself was named after the ancient city. The high land was free of the tsetse fly, which can cause cattle disease, so it was a good place for the Shona tribe to settle. The Shona were farmers and cattle herders. They counted wealth and importance by the number of cattle a group owned. The group of Shona living around Zimbabwe owned a lot of cattle, allowing them to give cattle as gifts to other Shona groups and so to secure their support and the help of their warriors. In this way, the Zimbabweans gained control of routes that led to the country's southwest, where the rocks and streams were rich in gold.

The Zimbabweans weren't all that keen on gold themselves. Instead, they traded it with others. They did make some jewelry out of gold, but they actually preferred decorations of copper and iron. However, on the east coast of Africa, Arab and Indian traders had come looking for gold. The Zimbabweans traded their gold and the ivory from local

The ruins of Great Zimbabwe that so puzzled early European explorers are still an awe-inspiring sight today.

elephants for things that they really wanted—beautiful cloth, glass beads, and fancy foreign pottery.

As the Zimbabweans became wealthier, they wanted to impress their neighbors by building an awe-inspiring capital. The layout was much like

that of a traditional Shona village, where a fence would enclose many round huts. Only instead of using wood and mud, the Zimbabweans built in stone. They used fire and water to crack the local granite into brick-sized slabs, which they then carefully laid together without mortar. The curving walls, thicker at the bottom than the top, sometimes rose more than thirty feet high. In places, the builders laid stone in decorative patterns, and they placed impressive columns and statues on the tops of walls.

Great Zimbabwe was not the only stone city the people built. *Zimbabwe* means "royal enclosure" or "stone buildings," and there were actually many smaller *zimbabwe*s built over a large area. In time, however, all the stone cities would be abandoned. Periods of low rainfall, political troubles, and overpopulation brought about the end of the *zimbabwe*s around 1500.

By the time Europeans arrived and began speculating about the Phoenicians and the Queen of Sheba, the Shona were back to living in wood-and-mud versions of *zimbabwe*s. But they knew who had really built the great stone towns—their own proud and powerful ancestors.

This painting of traders in a Shona city is based on evidence found in the ruins of Great Zimbabwe. In the background we can see one of the cone-shaped towers typical of Shona building styles.

THE ETHIOPIANS
A KING DIGS CHURCHES

Up until the year 1137 Ethiopia, in northeastern Africa, was ruled by the same royal family that had ruled for hundreds and hundreds of years. One reason this family stayed in power for so long was that it claimed to be descended from two famous figures mentioned in the Bible: King Solomon and the Queen of Sheba. This meant a lot to the people of Ethiopia, who had officially adopted the Christian religion in the year 340. In 1137, however, this family lost control of Ethiopia, and a new family, the Zagwes, took over.

The Zagwes claimed to be descended from Moses and his Ethiopian wife, who are mentioned even earlier in the Bible than King Solomon and the Queen of Sheba. Around 1200, however, one of the Zagwe rulers, King Lalibela, began to worry that his people doubted the truth of the Zagwe claim. So, to impress his people, King Lalibela began to build churches unlike any they had seen before. He didn't build them up; he built them down.

In one mountain town Lalibela had ten churches carved from the surface of

Seen from above, one of Lalibela's churches (left) looks like a gigantic cross. The cross is actually the roof of the church.

King Solomon and the Queen of Sheba meet for the first time in this painting by a modern Ethiopian artist. For centuries Ethiopia was ruled by a family whose claim to the throne was based on its descent from the famous monarchs.

the ground down into the red volcanic rock. Once the outside shape of the church was excavated, the inside was hollowed out. Pillars, altars, and windows were carved from the solid rock.

To impress his people even more, Lalibela said that God had taken him into heaven and shown him the plan for these churches. Legend said that God had even helped with the construction by sending angels to work on the buildings all night once the king's workers finished at sundown.

All this did not secure the kingship for Lalibela's family. Fifty years after the king died in 1220, the old royal family took over Ethiopia again. But the rock-hewn churches made by Lalibela remain among the most remarkable buildings in the world.

Pacific
Ocean

Rocky Mountains

N
W   E
S

Mesa Verde ●

Mississippi River

Atlantic
Ocean

Chichén
Itzá ●

Caribbean Sea

THE AMERICAS
AROUND 1200

Amazon River

Chan Chan ●   *Moche River*

Andes Mountains

Lake Titicaca

■ ANASAZI SETTLEMENTS
□ MAYAN LANDS
■ CHIMU EMPIRE

Miles   0   500   1000   1500
Kilometers   0   1000   2000

PART IV

THE AMERICAS

By 1200 humans had been in the Americas for at least 30,000 years, and a number of civilizations had already come and gone. Others were about to appear on the scene. Some would reach new heights before invaders from Europe would bring them to an end around 1500. Still, a look at the year 1200 shows an array of interesting civilizations with proud pasts and, as far as their people knew, promising futures.

WHEN THEY RULED
The Chimu Empire
around 1200—1470

Mesoamerica—The Late Period
around 900—1500

The Anasazi Culture
around 100—1350

THE CHIMU
THE CRAFTSPEOPLE OF PERU

When most people think of ancient Peru, they think of the Inca—the fabulous "Empire of the Sun," with its massive stone cities and its rulers resplendent in feathers and gold. We know a fair amount about the Inca, whose empire began about 1438, because of the descriptions written by Spanish conquerors in the 1500s. Even while destroying Incan civilization, the Spanish wrote about the conquered people's history and beliefs. Since then, archaeologists have added to the picture—a far richer picture than first thought.

The Inca were the final product of a long series of Peruvian cultures. Much of Incan religion, art, government, and architecture had been developed by earlier groups of people. One of these was the Chimu.

In 1200 the Chimu were the real power on the Peruvian scene. Their six-hundred-mile-long empire was tied together by roads over which armies moved and runners traveled, carrying official news. Chan Chan, a massive city located on Peru's coast, was the empire's capital.

The Chimu didn't have a writing system, but they kept records and sent orders by knotting colored cords, the same way the Inca later did. And like the Inca, they didn't always have to threaten war to expand their empire. They could offer their neighbors a chance to be part of a wealthy trade network from which they could get plentiful food and abundant, beautiful goods.

Around 1200 Chan Chan was the largest, most populous city in the Americas. It covered eight square miles and had a population of about 50,000. The city was a maze of pyramids, adobe-brick houses, and little apartments made of woven cane. Within the city the king lived in a walled smaller city with its own storerooms, quarters for craftspeople, kitchens, administrative offices, and burial platforms. When a king died, his

*This ancient paved road near Lake Titicaca in Peru was
one of the roads that held the vast Inca empire together. In 1200,
when the Inca were still a minor tribe, the Chimu Empire dominated
Peru. Features that we think of as typical of the Inca, such as
the huge network of roads and the system of runners carrying
news throughout the empire, were developed by the Chimu.*

successor would build his own royal mini-city. In this way, Chan Chan
developed at least ten of these cities-within-a-city.

The wealth of the Chimu was built not only on trade but on agriculture
and manufacturing as well. The Chimu turned their desert coastline into

*Today, ruins are all that remain of Chan Chan,
the capital of the great Chimu Empire.*

farmland by building irrigation canals, which carried water from the Moche River. The people had to be well organized not only to construct the canals but also to keep them clean and repaired. Fertile soil, called silt, would erode from the mountainsides and clog the canals as it enriched the farmland. Many workers were needed to keep the canals clean. The Chimu government required all its citizens to work for the public good. So people cleaned the canals, built and repaired roads, and fought in the imperial army.

Craftsmanship was valued among the Chimu. The government paid its many artisans with food, clothing, housing, and medical care. As a result, Chan Chan became a manufacturing center, producing a tremendous

The Chimu worked dazzling designs in gold. This tumi, a knife used to kill sacrificial victims, is made of gold and semi-precious stones.

Chimu pottery was both decorative and practical.

Many Chimu men wore earrings like these.

ALL-AMERICAN FEAST

If it had not been for the early Americans, menus everywhere would be a lot poorer. Many of the foods we take for granted today were native only to the Americas and spread throughout the world after Europeans arrived.

The Peruvians grew about two hundred varieties of potatoes. Potatoes are now a basic food, cultivated from Ireland to Russia to India. Tomatoes too are basic to cooking worldwide, and it's hard to imagine life without peanuts, corn chips, and chocolate—all foods that came to us from the early Americans. The Chimu and Inca were also fond of eating guinea pig.

Today you can easily put together a meal and tell your guests that their plates would be bare if it weren't for the Native Americans who first learned how to grow the foods you're serving. You might include potatoes, tomatoes, corn, chili peppers, bell peppers, squash, pineapple, kidney beans, and sweet potatoes. Feel free to skip the guinea pig.

amount of pottery, cloth, and metalwork. In fact, when the Inca finally conquered the Chimu, around 1470, they took many Chimu craftspeople to Cuzco, the Incan capital. These skilled workers then made jewelry, pottery, and textiles for the Incan nobility. They also taught the Inca these crafts and so helped strengthen the empire, for the abundance of manufactured goods encouraged other peoples to join the Inca.

It's likely that much of the fabulous Incan gold that so dazzled the Spanish was in fact the work of the Chimu.

THE MESOAMERICANS
MAKING PERFECT SACRIFICES

Around 1200 the great Mayan civilization that had dominated Meso-america* was coming to an end. Chichén Itzá, one of the last major Mayan cities, was largely destroyed around 1180. But there was one place in the city ruins that the Maya kept coming back to for years—through 1200 and beyond. This was the Well of Sacrifice, a huge natural sinkhole where Chac, the god of rainfall, was thought to dwell. For the farming Maya, rainfall was vital, and they would walk for miles to ask for it or for other

In the ruins of Chichén Itzá stands this building, the Temple of the Warriors. The statue in foreground is a Chac Mool, an altar used in ritual sacrifice. The hearts and entrails of victims were offered to the gods on the plate that the Chac Mool figure is holding.

For hundreds of years, giving sacrifices to the gods was a major part of Mayan culture. A main reason the Mayans went to war was to capture prisoners for sacrifice. This Mayan battle scene shows warriors raiding an enemy village.

favors from the god. Usually the people made an offering of something they valued, throwing it into the deep pool of water. It might be gold, jade, or pottery. Sometimes it was a child.

Mayan priests would select the most beautiful, perfect-seeming child. Then, at dawn on the appointed day, the boy or girl would be dressed in finery, with golden sandals and anklets of copper bells. After ceremonies in a temple beside the well, the child would be thrown in. Usually the victim sank to the cloudy bottom to be with Chac. But if by noon the sacrifice was still alive, the child was fished out and asked what prophetic message he or she had to deliver from the god.

No doubt it was a great honor to be chosen to help one's people. But there must have been moments when the chosen child wished for a slightly less perfect appearance, and a longer life.

*Mesoamerica means "middle America." The term refers to Central America and part of Mexico in the time before the coming of the Europeans.

THE ANASAZI
AMERICA'S FIRST APARTMENT DWELLERS

Apartment buildings, those tall buildings that we see so often in big cities and towns, are usually thought of as a modern type of dwelling. But, in the Americas at least, they aren't new at all. For the Anasazi, apartment buildings were standard.

By 1200 the Anasazi had already resided for more than a thousand years around the "four corners"—the area where the modern states of Arizona, New Mexico, Colorado, and Utah meet. We don't know what these people called themselves, but later when the Navajo moved into the area and found vast abandoned ruins, they called those earlier settlers Anasazi, or the "enemy ancestors."

The ruins were impressive. Around the year 1000 the Anasazi were mostly living on the tops of mesas or other open areas. They built pueblos, large apartment complexes of stone and adobe where many families lived in rooms next to or on top of one another.

The Anasazi were farmers who improved their dry lands by developing a clever irrigation system. On the rare occasions when rainstorms came, water that rushed off cliffs and out of side valleys was trapped in little reservoirs and diverted into channels that watered the fields of corn, beans, and squash. This worked so well that several planting cycles were possible each year.

By 1200, however, these farmers had moved their homes, although they kept their fields on the mesa tops or in valley bottoms. Perhaps the threat of warfare made the Anasazi seek more defensible places. Or maybe the need to feed a growing population convinced them they shouldn't build on good farmland. Many began building instead on the sides of cliffs,

These ruins at Mesa Verde, Colorado, are some of the most famous Anasazi cliff apartments. The round structures at the front of the picture are kivas, used for ceremonies. If you look closely, you can see ladders used to climb from one level of the pueblo to another.

tucking their homes into crevasses or under huge stone overhangs.

Some Anasazi pueblos had hundreds of rooms and rose four or five stories high. To get into or out of their apartments, people used wooden ladders or scrambled up the cliffs, using shallow handholds in the stone. Farmers climbed up and down daily to tend their fields, and accidents did happen, as is shown by the wooden crutches found in the ruins and the number of bodies with healed bones in Anasazi cemeteries.

Cliffside apartments offered protection from the climate as well as from enemies. In the winter, when the sun is low, the many south-facing dwellings received warm sunshine and protection from the north wind. In summer, when the sun is high, the overhanging cliffs shadowed the homes during the heat of the day. Thick walls of stone and adobe also helped to keep rooms warm in winter and cool in summer.

These rooms had narrow doors, no windows, and little furniture other than mats. When they were not farming, people spent most of their time outside in the plazas or on the roof. Men chipped tools from stone, women coiled clay into pots, and children played with pet turkeys and dogs.

Every village had at lease one kiva, a round room built partly underground that was entered through a hole in the roof. Here men met to talk about village affairs and perform religious rituals. Although the Anasazi had no writing system to record their beliefs, these were probably similar to the beliefs of modern-day Pueblo Indians. The Anasazi recognized their closeness to the land and the natural world. Their ceremonies in kivas and out in public may have included dancers dressed as ancestor or nature spirits.

Some Anasazi settlements such as Pueblo Bonito in Colorado's

This sixteen-inch-tall figure is typical of Anasazi pottery. The black and white painted patterns are one of the main ways we can recognize Anasazi pottery.

Everyday items like this vividly painted pottery bowl continue to be found all over Anasazi dwellings, making it seem as if their owners had left them behind only hours before.

Chaco Canyon, were thought particularly sacred. Religious festivals held there attracted pilgrims from great distances. Many Anasazi villages were linked by straight roads and a system of towers. Messages were sent from tower to tower by the lighting of signal beacons, by smoke, or by sunlight reflected from mirrors of shiny mica stone. The Anasazi also used the towers for studying the movements of the sun, moon, and planets. By observing

STONE VERSUS STEEL:
One Author's (Pam's) Observations

The Anasazi had no metal tools. Their knives, spear points, and arrowheads were made of stone. I used to think that sounded pretty primitive.

However, once when I was on an archaeological excavation in Arizona, an expert in Native American toolmaking paid us a visit. With swift tapping of stone hammer and bone awl, he turned lumps of obsidian into dozens of sharp flaked tools like the ones we were excavating. They looked good, but most of us figured that if we really needed a cutting tool, we'd take a modern steel knife.

Then one night a bear attacked some cattle nearby and was shot. Here was a perfect chance to test ideas about tools! We divided into two teams. My team would skin half the bear using the newly made stone tools. The other team would use modern steel knives. We would see who finished first.

None of us had ever skinned a bear before. We set to work, steel and obsidian blades flashing in the sun. Before we knew it, my team had won. Our obsidian blades were much sharper. They cut through the

where the light of the rising or setting sun fell on certain days, they could tell when to plant or harvest and when to hold important rituals.

But in time even the most sacred rituals were not enough. The Anasazi population, fed by the good farming system, became larger than the land could support. At the same time many years of below-average rainfall caused crops to fail. Because of these hardships Anasazi villages may have fought among themselves, and outside warriors may have been a threat as well.

tough bear hide as if cutting through butter. But, although we finished first, we had had to change blades several times. Whenever we hit a bone, our stone blades would break. The steel blades never broke. Steel was stronger than stone, but it wasn't as sharp.

Change, it seems, doesn't always mean that things get better—just different.

These Anasazi spears were found in Utah, complete with their original shafts and bindings.

By 1300 most Anasazi villages were deserted. The people, however, left behind so many everyday items, such as baskets and food, that is seems as if some Anasazi thought they were only leaving for a short time and would return. But they never did. They moved elsewhere and joined with other people. Today some Anasazi ways endure in the lives of Pueblo people such as the Hopi and Zuni. And ruins left by the "enemy ancestors" continue to impress visitors with the skill and vision of America's first apartment dwellers.

WORLD EVENTS AROUND 1200

1095—The First Crusade
1126—Jurchens conquer northern China
1137—The Zagwes take over Ethiopia
1141—Gaozong, first emperor of China's Southern Song dynasty, makes peace with the Jurchens
1147—Almohads conquer Islamic Spain
1148—Gaozong establishes Southern Song capital at Hangzhou
1160—Taira defeat the Minamoto clan in Japan
1173—Eleanor of Aquitaine and her sons rebel against Henry II; Eleanor is imprisoned
1180—Fall of Maya/Toltec city of Chichén Itzá
1185—Minamoto destroy the Taira
1187—Saladin captures Jerusalem
1189—Minamoto Yoshitsune commits suicide
——Henry II dies; Richard I becomes king of England
1192—Minamoto Yoritomo establishes Japan's first shogunate
1199—Minamoto Yoritomo dies
1200*
——Almohads control northwest Africa and Islamic Spain
——*Oni* of Ile Ife sends son to found royal dynasty of Benin
——Stone building at Zimbabwe is under way
——King Lalibala begins building rock-hewn churches of Ethiopia
——Chimu Empire dominates Peru
——Anasazi cliff dwellers flourish in the American southwest
1206—Temujin is declared Ghengis Khan, ruler of all the Mongols
1215—Mongols capture the Jurchen capital, Zhongdu, in northern China
1217–1263—Reign of Haakon IV, king of Norway
1219—Ghengis Khan captures Bukhara
1227—Ghengis Khan dies
1230*
——Snorri Sturluson writes the *Heimskringla*
1234—Mongols complete the conquest of northern China with help from the Southern Song
1241—Snorri Sturluson is murdered for supporting Icelandic independence
1252–1284—Reign of Alfonso X, El Sabio, in Spain
1271—Mongols capture Hangzhou
1279—Mongols defeat the last Southern Song resistance and establish a new dynasty in China

*dates approximate

GLOSSARY

adobe A building material made of sun-dried earth and straw.

Berber An ethnic group native to North Africa since the first century B.C. For centuries, many Berber tribes were nomadic herders.

brass A mixture of copper and zinc, harder than pure copper and shinier than bronze.

bronze A mixture of copper and tin, harder than pure copper or brass.

Buddhist A follower of Buddhism, a religion that began in India in the sixth century B.C. and spread to China, Japan and other countries of the Far East.

Christian A follower of Christianity, a religion based on the belief that Jesus Christ was the Son of God.

clan A group of families that are related to one another.

Crusade One of the wars fought by Christians in the eleventh to thirteenth centuries to capture the Holy Land from the Muslims.

dynasty A series of rulers from a single family.

inoculation A substance that contains weakened disease germs, which is given to a person to help the body protect itself against the disease.

Islam A religion originating in seventh century Arabia. Its five essential duties are acknowledging the supremacy of Allah (God) and Muhammad as his prophet, praying five times daily, fasting in the month of Ramadan, going on pilgrimage to Mecca in Arabia some time in one's life, and devoting a portion of one's resources to helping the needy.

Jew A follower of Judaism, a religion based on the belief that there is only one God, who revealed himself to Abraham, Moses, and the ancient Hebrew prophets.

Koran The holy book of the Islamic religion, containing the teachings of the prophet Muhammad.

leprosy A disease that can destroy flesh and nerves, greatly feared in the medieval period. People with leprosy were usually isolated from the rest of society.

liberal Supportive of new ideas, particularly in politics and religion.

mesa A flat-topped mountain, from the Spanish word for "table."

monasteries Religious centers lived in by monks. In many cultures monasteries have also served as schools and universities.

monk A man who has vowed to live a religious life. Monks often live in isolation from the rest of society and are not allowed to marry.

mosque An Islamic place of worship.

Muslim A follower of the Islamic religion.

naginata A spear with a long curved blade, the traditional weapon of Japanese warrior monks.

nomads People who live in different places throughout the year, moving seasonally to find better conditions for their animals, rather than living in one permanent location.

Norse Having to do with the people or language of early Scandinavia. The early Scandinavian language is known as Old Norse.

nun A woman who has vowed to live a religious life. Nuns usually live in isolation from the rest of society and are not allowed to marry.

obsidian A dark natural glass formed by the cooling of volcanic lava.

pilgrimage A trip taken by a religious believer to a holy place.

ransom Money paid to free someone who has been captured.

rituals A series of standardized actions performed in a fixed way, often as part a of religious ceremony.

Sabbath A day of the week set aside for rest and worship.

saga An old Icelandic story about early Scandinavian heroes.

samurai The warrior class in medieval Japan.

Saracens A term for the Arabs, used by the people of medieval Europe.

Scandinavia A region in northwestern Europe, made up of the countries Denmark, Norway, Sweden, Finland, and Iceland.

skald An early Scandinavian poet.

sultan A Muslim ruler.

synagogue A Jewish place of worship, sometimes known as a temple.

tournament A form of combat popular in medieval Europe as a sport and as training for war.

tribute Payment a country makes to a foreign ruler.

Viking One of the Scandinavian pirates who raided the coasts of Europe in the eighth to tenth centuries. Scholars think that the word *Viking* (from the Old Norse for "bay" or "creek") came from the fact that these pirates' shallow-bottomed ships allowed them to sail right up onto the beaches of bays and up creeks that were too shallow for most other ships.

FOR FURTHER READING

Adeeb, Hassan, and Bonetta Adeeb. *Nigeria: One Nation, Many Cultures.* New York: Marshall Cavendish, 1996.

Anda, Michael O. *Yoruba.* New York: Rosen Publishing, 1996.

Blashfield, Jean F. *Norway.* New York, Children's Press, 2000.

Brill, Marlene Targ. *Mongolia.* Chicago: Children's Press, 1992.

Brooks, Polly Schoyer. *Queen Eleanor, Independent Spirit of the Medieval World: A Biography of Eleanor of Acquitane.* New York: J.B. Lippincott, 1983.

Child, John. *The Rise of Islam.* New York: Peter Bedrick Books, 1995.

Demi. *Chingis Khan.* New York: Henry Holt, 1991.

Fisher, Leonard Everett. *Anasazi.* New York: Atheneum Books for Young Readers, 1997.

Fradin, Dennis. *Ethiopia.* Chicago: Children's Press, 1994.

Galvin, Irene Flum. *The Ancient Maya.* New York: Marshall Cavendish, 1997.

Greenblatt, Miriam. *Genghis Khan and the Mongol Empire.* New York: Marshall Cavendish, 2002.

Hallam, Elizabeth, ed. *The Plantagenet Chronicles.* New York: Weidenfeld and Nicolson, 1986.

Hinds, Kathryn. *The Incas.* New York: Marshall Cavendish, 1998.

——. *The Vikings.* New York: Marshall Cavendish, 1998.

Koslow, Philip. *Centuries of Greatness, 750–1900: West African Kingdoms.* New York: Chelsea House, 1995.

Martell, Hazel Mary. *Native Americans and Mesa Verde.* New York: Dillon Press, 1993.

McLenighan, Valjean. *China, a History to 1949.* Chicago: Children's Press, 1983.

Millar, Heather. *The Kingdom of Benin in West Africa.* New York: Marshall Cavendish, 1997.

Perl, Lila. *Ethiopia, Land of the Lion.* New York: William Morrow, 1972.

Sattler, Helen Roney. *The Earliest Americans.* New York: Clarion, 1993.

Schomp, Virginia. *Japan in the Days of the Samurai.* New York: Marshall Cavendish, 2002.

Sheehan, Sean. *Zimbabwe.* New York: Marshall Cavendish, 1993.

Shinnie, Margaret. *Ancient African Kingdoms*. New York: St. Martin's Press, 1965.

Steck-Vaughn Company. *Civilization of the Americas*. Austin, TX: Steck-Vaughn, 1992.

Stuart, Gene S. *America's Ancient Cities*. Washington, DC: National Geographic Society, 1988.

Van Wyck, Gary N., and Robert Johnson, Jr. *Shona*. New York: Rosen Publishing, 1997.

Wilcox, Jonathan. *Iceland*. New York: Marshall Cavendish, 1996.

Wood, Marion. *Ancient America*. Oxford: Facts on File, 1990.

ON-LINE INFORMATION*

http://www.lysator.liu.se/nordic/scn/faq53
.html
Information on Icelandic history, with links
to information on Scandinavian history

http://www.womeninworldhistory.com/
heroine2.html
A site with information on Eleanor of
Aquitaine and other women in world history

http://www.mongols.com
The history, culture, people, and art
of Mongolia

http://www.pantheon.org
Information about different mythologies

http://www.fa.indiana.edu/~conner/
yoruba/cut.html
Overview of the Yoruba people and
Yoruba art

http://www.uiowa.edu/~africart/toc/people/
A site about African cultures and art

http://www.beloit.edu/~museum/logan/
catalog/samerica/peru/ancient/chimu/
#artifacts
A site maintained by the Logan Museum
of Anthropology, with information about
and images of Chimu art

http://www.utep.edu/region19/modules/
natast05/html/natast11.htm
Information on the Anasazi and other early
cultures of the southwestern United States

http://mcclungmuseum.utk.edu/specex/
maya/maya.htm
Photos and additional information
on Mayan art

www.sci.mus.mn.us/sln/ma/index.html
Information on Mayan culture with photos,
maps, activities and related links. Sponsored
by the Science Museum of Minnesota

*Websites change from time to time. For
additional on-line information, check with
the media specialist at your local library.

ABOUT THE AUTHORS

Mother and daughter writing team Pam
and Alex Service share an interest in
history, writing, and theater.

Pam holds a master's degree in African
history from the University of London.
She has been a history museum curator for
nearly twenty years, first in Bloomington,
Indiana, and currently in Eureka,
California. She is the author of eighteen
books for young people. This is her third
for Benchmark Books.

Alex developed an early interest in
history. In school she wrote several award-
winning plays set in historical times. For
her bachelor's degree, from UCLA, she
studied Japanese history and culture. She
recently completed a doctorate program in
medieval studies at the University of York
in England and is now the director of a
history museum in Thermopolis, Wyoming.

INDEX